My Name: _______________ Date: _____________

My Personal Discovery and Growth Guidebook
During Pregnancy and Childbirth

Expecting Moms Edition

Find more resources to treasure God, yourself, and your family at:

https://treasuringyourunbornchild.com

ISBN 978-1-963227-37-6

Other upcoming books in the *Treasuring Your Unborn Child —A Legacy of Love During Pregnancy and Childbirth* series:

Expecting Moms
Expecting Dads
Expecting Couples
Expecting Grandparents

This book is published by Transforming Life Press LLC, Kissimmee, FL USA through Amazon KDP. Visit transforminglifepress.com for more titles.

Also by Dave Pipitone,
The Rainbow Chronicles: A Story of Hope for Today, Third Edition
I Treasure God Prayer Journals
Treasured in My Heart: Talking, Singing, and Writing to Your Loved Ones in Paradise (24 titles)
Treasured in My Heart: Connecting with Your Loved One in Paradise, Military/Veterans (10 titles)
A Song Without End
Rose of My Heart
(Available on Amazon.com)

Acknowledgments
Thanks go to Cheryl and Emily Pipitone; Atif from Pakistan for graphic design work; Janice Barrett; Chloé Battle, Bob Perron and the staff of JMJ Pregnancy Center, Kissimmee, FL; Rihanna Curtis and Mariah David for their excellent singing, and the mustard seed for Living Epiphany planted by Fr. Patrick J. Brennan and Dawn Mayer.

Table of Contents

Living Epiphany: Treasuring Begins

"On entering the house they saw the child with Mary his mother. They prostrated themselves and did him homage. Then they opened their treasures and offered him gifts of gold, frankincense and myrrh." Matthew 2:11

The Gospel of Matthew in the Bible tells the story of The Epiphany. Magi from the east come to Israel seeking a newborn king. They find the infant Jesus in Bethlehem and opened their treasures to honor him. The magi gave three gifts of gold, frankincense and myrrh–a treasury kept by parents Mary and Joseph.

Treasuring is about honoring. Honoring another person is the outward sign of a treasuring heart. Honoring involves deep respect. Jesus honored His Father and His disciples. Joseph and Mary honored each other, God's work in their lives, and their child Jesus–before and after birth. The magi did Jesus homage and honored Him with three gifts from their treasures.

God honored you before you were born with three treasures by creating you in God's Divine Image. God continues to honor you every day of your life on earth and in heaven afterwards. Living epiphany means treasuring God, yourself, and other people.

Made in God's Divine Image

This *Guidebook* is about the middle strand of Living Epiphany: treasuring you!

Every human being is created in God's Divine Image, after God's Likeness, as shown in the Bible verses below. The first story of creation in very first chapter of Genesis, the first book of the Bible contains these words. According to that story, God saved the best for last–creating human beings as the crown of creation. You are very good in God's eyes.

God has made you in God's Divine Image and God is making your baby in the Divine Image too. There are three treasures that flow from God's Divine Image: the Treasure of Being, the Treasure of Doing, and the Treasure of Sharing.

God is the source of all life–the treasure of all being. Right now, God is giving existence to your baby with and through you.

God is the Creator, the source of all doing, Who does all things. Right now, with God's help, your body is doing God's work of creating your baby's body.

God is the source of all sharing, living together in a community of three loving Persons–the Father, Jesus the Son, and the Holy Spirit. Right now, you are sharing life with God and your baby through every heartbeat.

God has given you the gift of life and is working with and through you to bring a new life to the world. That life is starting in your womb as an unborn child. When your baby is born, you will be, do, and share life with your child as he/she grows and develops.

> *"Then God said, 'Let us make human beings in our image, after our likeness.' God created mankind in His image; in the image of God He created them; male and female God created them. God looked at everything He had made and found it very good."*
>
> *Genesis 1:26a, 27, 31a*

A Treasure That Keeps Growing

During your life and pregnancy, you will experience many epiphanies. Epiphany means manifestation–like a secret being revealed.

Human beings discover what God uncovers. God reveals His love over time because we can't take it all in all at once. In fact, it will take forever to come to know God's love. So, don't try to cram in the learning. You have plenty of time.

During your pregnancy journey, you will discover the wonder of a new human life that God is creating with you during nine months. You will have the honor of sharing a child with your family, a new person of tremendous value that never existed before without you.

The wonderful news is that God will continue to bless your treasures and those of your family. What are those treasures of yours, anyway? Turn the page and start discovering!

Rediscover Your Three Treasures

As you go through pregnancy, now is a wonderful time to get in touch with the three treasures that God has given you. This will help you to admire yourself, encourage yourself, and appreciate how God has gifted you in your life. When you are in touch with your own three treasures of being, doing, and sharing, you will develop a greater honor for yourself. You will have greater respect for life. It will be easier to recognize the unique design of other people and their treasures when you know your own. By the end of this Guidebook, you will be able to say "I treasure me!" more easily.

When all the treasures of all people are added up, we can see a glimpse God's glory alive in the human race. St. Peter compares the people of God to living stones. We are diamonds that grow. The Book of Revelation uses vivid imagery of the New Jerusalem, a symbol of heaven, as a city built on twelve layers of precious stones. You are an important part of God's work and the great treasure God has been creating since the beginning of time.

Your Gifts are the Facets of Your Treasures

Let's explore the three treasures you have now and that continue to grow. Pages 8-18 contain a simple way to unearth, mine, and discover your three treasures of being, doing, and sharing. Each of your three treasures is shown as a diamond with many facets. Think of the diamond as a precious jewel. The facets are how the "sparkle" of the diamond shines out. Facets are flat surfaces that a jeweler cuts to let new light inside. That light is reflected inside the diamond to give the fire and sparkle to the gem. God is the One who gave you the three treasures. God created your gifts and gave them to you to make you the dazzling person that you are. God's light is what makes your life sparkle. Your experiences and relationships in life help shape these gifts.

The light of God's love reflecting inside you makes you sparkle!

Your First Assignments

You are going on a treasuring hunt for your three treasures. Turn to next section, *Your Three Treasures*. Read the first page about each Treasure. Then, go to the following page, look at the list, select and rank the gifts (or facets) that you see in yourself. If you need help, say a prayer to ask God for insight, or meet with a friend who knows you. Start with the *Treasure of Being*. After you complete it, use the same process to uncover *Your Treasure of Doing* and *Your Treasure of Sharing*. Take your time with this personal discovery. You will discover the wonderful, loving, lovely, and beloved woman and mother that you are. Your love will grow for God, yourself, your baby, and other people.

Your Three Treasures

Your Treasure of Being

Your treasure of being includes all those gifts that lie at the core of your personality and existence. God is the source of all being. God gave you life when God created you.

Your life, personality, and all the elements of your person started in your mother's womb. It took years after you were born to grow into the fullness of these gifts. If you've never discovered all of the gifts that God has placed in your treasure of being, now is a good time.

Some facets of your treasure of being include:

- Your physical traits like body size and shape; skin, eye, and hair color; your unique fingerprints, voice pattern; and more.
- Your learning style: visual, auditory, or kinesthetic.
- Your personality tendencies, like introvert/extrovert, and more.
- Your aptitudes or natural gifts, like structural or abstract thinking, pitch discrimination, color perception, and more.
- Your heritage and genes that spring from previous generations.
- Your soul and consciousness, that God creates and makes you a unique human being.

Now is the time to discover your treasure of being on a deeper level. See the next page to get started.

Unearthing Your Treasure of Being

Read through the following partial list of words. Select as many of these personality traits that you have developed. Rate how strong you are at that trait, using a scale of 1 to 10; *10=Very Strong 0=Definitely Not Me*. Circle anything above 0. Use the blank lines to add traits not listed here.

	Accepting		Excited		Patient
	Accountable		Expansive		Passionate
	Adorable		Faithful		Persistent
	Attentive		Fearless		Poised
	Aware		Focused		Positive
	Balanced		Forgiving		Powerful
	Beautiful		Free		Praising
	Blessing		Generous		Persevering
	Bold		Gentle		Productive
	Brave		Giving		Protecting
	Calm		Grateful		Purposeful
	Caring		Guiding		Radiant
	Centered		Happy		Receptive
	Charitable		Harmonious		Sacred
	Committed		Healing		Serving
	Community		Honest		Sincere
	Compassionate		Hopeful		Stable
	Confident		Humble		Still
	Conscientious		Humorous		Strong
	Considerate		Illuminating		Supportive
	Constructive		Innocent		Temperate
	Cooperative		Inspiring		Tolerant
	Courageous		Intelligent		Transforming
	Creative		Intuitive		Trusting
	Dedicated		Joyful		Trustworthy
	Determined		Just		Truthful
	Devoted		Kind		Uplifting
	Dignified		Leading		Victorious
	Diligent		Listening		Wise
	Diplomatic		Loving		Worthy
	Discerning		Loyal		
	Disciplined		Magnetic		
	Dynamic		Merciful		
	Elegant		Motivating		
	Empathetic		Non-Judgmental		
	Empowering		Observing		
	Enlightened		Open		

The Facets (Gifts) in My Treasure of Being

From page 10, write the facets of your personality and personal traits God has given you in the space around the diamond below. Now, imagine God holding the jewel of your *Treasure of Being* in His hand. God raises the jewel of you, your soul, your personality, physical traits, and more into the sunlight of His love to admire beauty that He has created.

"I will give you treasures of darkness, and riches hidden away, that you may know that I am the LORD, the God of Israel, who calls you by name." Isaiah 45:3

Your Treasure of Doing

Your treasure of doing includes all those gifts that lie at the core of your ability to direct and control the actions of your body and mind.

Your physical and mental abilities started to develop when you were in your mother's womb. After you were born, you learned to use your body and your mind to do different things. You learned to eat with a spoon, tie your shoes, and do many other things.

You learn something new every day. Now is the time remember what some of your skills and talents are.

As a mom, you will have the privilege and honor to help your baby unearth, develop, and grow this treasure.

Some facets of your treasure of doing include:

- Your physical mobility, flexibility, balance, capacity for strength, and more.
- Your capacity for activity, including focus, concentration, and planning.
- Your capacity to coordinate your mind and body.
- Your mastery for doing certain things.
- The specific skills and talents you have developed.
- Your capacity to learn and do things that come naturally to you.

You can learn to do many new things throughout your life. As a mom, you receive the ability to help your child to develop and protect her/his treasure of doing for a full and happy life.

Discovering Your Valuable Facets of Doing

Select as many of these skills and talents that you have developed. Rate how good you are at that skill, using a scale of 1 to 10; 10=Mastered; 0=Terrible. Circle anything above 0. Use the blank lines to add skills or talents not listed here.

	Acting		Dog grooming		Pottery
	Aerobics		Dolls		Praying
	Aquarium		Drawing		Quilting
	Archery		Driving		Racket sports
	Astronomy		Embroidery		Reading
	Backpacking		Exercising		Restoring antiques
	Badminton		Fashion design		Running
	Baking		Fencing		Sailing
	Ballet		Fishing		Scrap booking
	Basket Weaving		Flowers		Scripture groups
	Bead work		Gardening		Sculpting
	Bird Watching		Genealogy		Sewing
	Board Games		Golf		Shopping
	Book Club		Guitar		Singing
	Bowling		Gymnastics		Skiing
	Bridge		Hair dressing		Speaking
	Butterfly Watching		Hiking		Stained glass
	Cake decorating		Home making		Star gazing
	Camping		Horse riding		Sunning
	Canoeing		Ice Skating		Surfing
	Candle making		Jogging		Swimming
	Card games		Karate		Tai Chi
	Care giving		Kayaking		Talking
	Cartoons		Knitting		Teaching
	Chatting		Landscaping		Traveling
	Church groups		Leading		Volunteering
	Coaching		Listening to Music		Walking
	Collecting		Martial arts		Weaving
	Conservation		Meditating		Wine tasting
	Cooking		Nature		Writing
	Crafting		Nutrition		
	Crocheting		Organizing events		
	Crosswords		Painting		
	Cupcakes		Parenting		
	Cycling		Pet care		
	Dancing		Photography		
	Decorating		Playing music		

The Facets (Gifts) in My Treasure of Doing

From page 13, write the facets of your strengths and skills God has given you in the space around the diamond below. Now, imagine God holding the jewel of your *Treasure of Doing* in His hand. God raises the jewel of you, your talents, and skills into the sunlight of His love to admire beauty that He has created.

"You shall be glorious crown in hand of the LORD, a royal diadem in the hand of your God." Isaiah 62:3

Your Treasure of Sharing

Your treasure of sharing includes all those gifts that lie at the core of your ability to form relationships with God, the world and people around you.

Sharing is being and doing *together.*

Your sharing abilities began in your mother's womb.

Your relationship with God began the moment God thought of creating you.

Your first relationship with a human being was with your mother, then others who talked with your mother and you. After you were born, you began to meet, know, play and work with others. As an expecting mom, you will have the privilege and honor to help your baby develop and grow this treasure.

Some facets (gifts) of your Treasure of Sharing include:

- Your ability to learn and use your five physical senses like sight, hearing, touch, taste, and smell. It is through these senses that you gather information about your environment and people.

- Your capacity to receive love from God, yourself, and others. You developed your beliefs about safety, security, feeling wanted, and loved during your experience in your mother's womb and with other people after birth.

- Your capacity to give love, based on your feelings of love received during your life and your decisions and actions to love others.

- Your very beginning perceptions of what is possible and safe to share.

As an expecting mom, you receive the ability to help your child develop and protect her/his treasure of sharing for a full and happy life. Studies by leading psychologies show that long term happiness comes from stable and loving relationships. Your unborn child's very first relationship with a human being is with you.

Mining Your Treasure of Sharing

Think about the important people in your life. Include yourself on that list. Who else comes to mind? How are they related to you? What are their names? How close are they to you? Use the space below to fill out that list.

Roles: God, Jesus, Mary, Joseph, Saints, Partner/Spouse, Child (Son/Daughter) Parent (Mom/Dad), Sibling (Brother/Sister), Relative (Aunt, Uncle, Nephew, Niece, Cousin), Friend, Other.

Closeness: Intimate (live together, known each other for a long time), Trusted, Casual, Distant.

Role	Name	Closeness
		Intimate Trusted Casual Distant
		Intimate Trusted Casual Distant
		Intimate Trusted Casual Distant
		Intimate Trusted Casual Distant
		Intimate Trusted Casual Distant
		Intimate Trusted Casual Distant
		Intimate Trusted Casual Distant
		Intimate Trusted Casual Distant
		Intimate Trusted Casual Distant
		Intimate Trusted Casual Distant
		Intimate Trusted Casual Distant
		Intimate Trusted Casual Distant
		Intimate Trusted Casual Distant
		Intimate Trusted Casual Distant
		Intimate Trusted Casual Distant
		Intimate Trusted Casual Distant

The Gift of People in My Treasure of Sharing

From page 16, write the names of the people God has put into your life in the space around the diamond below. Now, imagine God holding the jewel of your *Treasure of Sharing* in His hand. God raises the jewel of you and these people into the sunlight of His love to admire beauty that He has created.

"You are precious in my eyes and honored and I love you." *Isaiah 43:4*

Counting Up Your Treasures: It's All Love

Congratulations!

You've taken the time to live epiphany–to discover what God has uncovered, or revealed, to you. You are precious to God. God's love for you gives you the grace to become loving, lovely, and beloved.

During the journey of life, you will continue to discover three things: You are loving. You are lovely. You are beloved. And so will your child become. Love is more than just feelings. Love involves a decision to give up some things for the sake of something better. Giving up does not mean quitting. Giving up means going up and growing up–deciding to put others in your relationships before yourself.

You are Loving!
Loving is sacrificing. During pregnancy, you may have to give up a slim waistline. You may have to endure morning sickness, cramps, brain fogginess, and more, however short or long they last. You may have to rest more when you want to go out with your friends. You may have to give up some of your favorite foods that aren't good for your baby or give up an unhealthy habit like smoking or drinking alcoholic beverages. Listen to your body, your intuition, your doctor, and your baby. At the end of your pregnancy journey, you will be giving again–giving birth to your baby.

You are Lovely!
In fact, you are more beautiful than you can imagine. God's love makes you lovely. When you use all of the gifts in your treasures of being, doing, and sharing, you are shining with God's glory. God is the source of all beauty–and God's beauty is in you.

You are Beloved!
Throughout life, your feelings will be like a roller coaster. One minute, you feel exuberant. The next, you might feel anxious or depressed. That is normal. You will have good days and you will have not-so-good days. You are more than those feelings. No matter how or what you feel, you are beloved by God. God your Father loves you, Jesus loves you, and the Holy Spirit loves you. You are precious to God and God loves <u>you</u>. Remind yourself to read the Bible passages at the bottom of pages 11, 14, and 17 over and over.

Activity One: How Great Thou Art
How Great Thou Art is a beloved hymn about God's power, grace, and love that is based on a poem written in German by Carl Boberg in 1885. Listen to a special pregnancy version of this song at treasuringyourunbornchild.com/howgreatthouart. Then, go to page 19 and write your own words to God for creating you in God's Divine Image and giving the Treasures of Being, Doing, and Sharing to you.

Activity 1: How Great Thou Art for Being

Think of all of the awesome things in nature that God has made–things you can see or are invisible. Use the space below to write as many things as you think are amazing. Draw a picture or two of something you find beautiful. Write your name, too!

Scan the QR Code with your mobile device to listen to the marvelous Song, *The Great Dream of God*, which is about the pregnancy of Mary and the birth of Jesus.

An angel came, to speak these words to Mary
"Hail blessed one, full of heavenly grace.
The Lord's with you, favored are you among women,
To bear a Son, to save the human race.

And she sang "Yes, My Lord may Your will be."
How great Thou art, How great Thou art.
"Behold I come, let it be done to me."
How great Thou art, how great Thou art.

When in a dream, an angel said to Joseph,
"Be not afraid, take Mary into your home.
By the Spirit, she waits to bear a Savior,
To forgive sins, and bring our God's shalom."

And he awoke, taking Mary as his wife.
How great Thou art, How great Thou art.
He bore the yoke, he served the Bread of Life,
How great Thou art, How great Thou art.

And then they went, traveling to Bethlehem,
And found no room, the inn was filled to burst.
Yet a stable, where cows and chickens mingled,
Born from her womb, where Jesus breathed his first.

The Son of God, born in a lowly place.
How great Thou art, How great Thou art.
It may seem odd, God with a human face.
How great Thou art, How great Thou art.

Then angels sang to those in fields staying
Glad news have we, great joy, no more a stranger.
Today is born, in the city of David,
The Messiah, lying in a manger.

Glory to God! And peace to all on earth.
How great Thou art, How great Thou art.
Glory to God! A Savior at His birth.
How great Thou art, How great Thou art.

"Then sings my soul, my Savior God to Thee, how great Thou art, how great Thou art..."

Activity 2: Treasuring Hands for Doing

God created every part of your body so that you can do things in life. Trace your right or left hand in the space below. Look at your list on page 14, *Your Treasure of Doing*. On each finger that you draw, write down at least one thing you can do with your hands. Then, in the bottom square, draw your one of your baby's hands. Write at least three things you would like your baby to do with his/her hands.

Activity 3: Loving Hearts for Sharing

Sharing is being and doing together. God gave you a heart to love God, yourself and other people. Draw a large heart in the space below. Inside the heart, write down at least three things from your list of gifts in *Your Treasure of Being* on page 11 that you can share with others. From page 14, write two things you can do with others. From *Your Treasure of Sharing* on page 17, write down the names of two other people. Then, in the bottom square, draw a picture of your baby's heart. Write at least three ways you would like your baby to be and do with you and other people.

Your Three Strands: A Lifeline to God

There is Strength in Numbers
"A three-ply cord is not easily broken." You have a lifeline–a love line–that connects you to God that is made of three strands. Those three strands are faith, hope, and love. All three strands are God's gift to honor you and help you stay connected to God.

Faith helps you believe God is with you. Hope helps you expect to receive the good things God is making and doing for you. God's love helps you become the loving, lovely, and beloved woman and mother that you are.

Just like your baby's umbilical cord, your love line of faith, hope, and love will grow bigger and stronger throughout life. Your connection to God will become stronger and thicker each day unless you choose to cut the love line.

God wants you and your baby to be happy and healthy, full of love, life, and light. After birth, your baby will grow to live independently and will have his/her own relationship with God. Your child will have a lifeline of faith, hope, and love that is independent of yours. You will help your child grow in faith, hope, and love. Love is the greatest of these three strands. Love is the guiding force on your pregnancy journey.

There are three persons in every human relationship: yourself, another person, and God. God exists in Three Persons: the Father, Jesus the Son, and the Holy Spirit. During your pregnancy, you can nourish your love line to God through your prayers, your words, and your songs. Your love will grow and your baby will learn about God's love through you.

You have an awesome role as a mom. You are awesome! Take care of your three strands of faith, hope, and love. Keep them intact. They are your lifeline–and your love line–for a blessed life for you and your baby. To remind yourself, read the *My 3 Strands for Moms* prayer that is below. Now, turn to page 23 to do Activity 4.

My 3 Strands for Moms Prayer

A child and mother,
with God's hands,
knit a union of 3 Strands.
Three cords of love, faith, and hope
weave a tighter bond than rope.
One great love, a braid of three,
formed by God, my child and me.
May my 3 Strands be always near;
my child, my gift with God is here.

Activity 4: Your Three Strands

Take three strands of different colored thread or yarn. Each strand is fragile and easy to break by itself if you pull hard enough. Braid the three strands together into a cord. Now, try to break the braided cord. It's harder. Draw a picture of your three strands of faith, love and hope in the space below. In the square at the bottom of the page, draw a picture of the three strands in your baby's umbilical cord–two arteries and a vein. God has already knit the three strands of faith, love, and hope into your baby's soul.

Saying Beautiful, Loving Words to Yourself

Use the words in this list when you talk to God, yourself, and your baby. Circle the words that feel right to describe you. Then, say these words in simple sentences to yourself and baby. The next page has several simple sentences you can say. Add your own loving words in the space under My Special Words.

Adorable
Amazing
Astonishing
Astounding
Awesome
Beautiful
Beloved
Breathtaking
Brilliant
Charming
Cherished
Cute
Darling
Dazzling
Delightful
Dear to me
Engaging
Excellent
Exquisite
Extraordinary
Fabulous
Fair
Fantastic
Fascinating
Gentle
Good-looking
Gorgeous
Graceful
Grand
Incredible
Lovable
Lovely
Loving
Magnificent
Marvelous
Nice
Outstanding
Pleasing
Precious
Pretty
Priceless
Remarkable
Such a sweet heart
Sweet
Sweetheart
Terrific
Tremendous
Wonderful
Wondrous

My Special Words

Activity 5: Admiring Sentences

Look at the list of beautiful, loving words on page 24. Pick one word and use that word in one of these sentences. (Or make up your own sentence.)

Write a sentence in the *I Treasure Me* section in your copy of *Treasuring Your Born Child: Creating a Legacy During Pregnancy and Childbirth*. What do you treasure about yourself? Then, read or speak your words out loud to yourself. Use your name and smile as you say the words!

___________, I think you are so _____________________!

Wow! How ________________ I am! Thank you God for making and loving me!

I am so happy because God made me _______________!

I am _______________! Hooray!

I look, feel, and believe that I am ___________!

I love being ____________!

Today, I am going to be more ____________.

I feel good about being _____________.

I am made in God's likeness and Divine Image. That must make God _____________.

<u>*Your Own Sentences*</u>

"I have the strength for everything through Him Who empowers me."

Corinthians 4:13

Activity 6: I Got This!

You can do it! No matter how you feel or what is happening around you, you have the strength, the heart, and the courage to make it through the moment. God is an encouraging God, who empowers and blesses you. God created you, calls you, and strengthens you to grow and do good things throughout your entire life.

Think of something you need to do today, and feel unsure of doing. Say these sentences out loud to encourage and give heart to yourself. Ask God for strength. Then, get started with doing!

I can grow better today.

With God's strength, help and grace, I can do this!

I got this! Thank You, God!

I can become a loving, lovely, and beloved mom.

With God empowering me, I can do what it takes to enjoy this special day of life for me, my family, and my baby.

I can take today one moment at a time.

I can make it through ____________________ today.

God gave me the heart to do what it takes to have a good day, and I am acting on that!

I can take the best care of my body so that my baby will be healthy.

I can become more patient with the pace of pregnancy.

<u>Write Your Own Encouraging Sentences Below</u>

"Can mother forget her infant, be without tenderness for the child of her womb? Even should she forget, I will never forget you. See, upon the palms of My hands I have engraved you."

Isaiah 49:15-16

Activity 7: I Am Unforgettable!

God remembers you! Your capacity for giving and receiving love, respect, goodwill, and support are part of God's treasure of sharing to you. God prizes you as a valuable part of God's family. You belong. You count. Your life matters. Your life is important. God will never forget you. You and your baby mean the world to God.

Stand in front of a mirror and say these sentences to yourself out loud. Allow yourself to feel wanted, especially by God.

I am important to God, my baby and my family.

I'm proud of the loving woman and mother I am becoming.

God is creating this wonderful new life inside me with my genes and my body. I am so blessed.

God loves me. I love myself. I love my baby. I love my family.

My life matters. I count.

God made only one me and I'm glad I am me.

I mean the world to my baby and my family. God's love makes that happen.

I'm having an awesome day, that reflects the awesome person God made me to be.

I feel excited to receive and give God's love to others.

I look forward to sharing my baby with my family.

Activity 8: God Has My Life in His Hands

Jesus called Himself the Good Shepherd and told His disciples, *"My Father, Who has given them (Jesus' followers) to me is greater than all, and no one can take them out of the Father's hand."* (John 10:29.) You are engraved on the palms of God's hands, Who will never let go of you. (See page 28.) Write your name in the middle of the palm of Jesus below, and tape a copy of your baby's ultrasound picture to it, too.

God and Mary Sing to Me!

"Ah, you are beautiful, my beloved, ah, you are beautiful."
Song of Songs, 4:1

Listen to God's and Mary's Love Songs

How do you feel when someone sings Happy Birthday to you? Or Happy Anniversary? Or another song to celebrate <u>you</u>?

The reason people sing to you is because they love, respect, and honor you. The same thing is true of God. God sings to you all the time. God is rejoicing over you. God is prizing you. God is treasuring you.

Read this Bible verse from the Book of the Prophet Zephaniah:

"The Lord your God is in your midst, a mighty savior; he will rejoice over you with gladness and renew you in his love, God will sing joyfully because of you, as one sings at festivals." (Zephaniah 3:17)

God is always glad to be with you. God is a Friend Who will never let you down, forget about you, or abandon you. Not only that, God is full of joy because you exist. God made you to share life forever with Him and all those God has created.

Mary, the Mother of Jesus, is your spiritual mother, and your baby's spiritual mother, too. Listen to the songs that Mary would sing to you and your unborn child.

One very good way to celebrate God's love for you, is to celebrate yourself! How? By letting yourself, be admired, encouraged, and appreciated that you are wonderfully made by God.

The following pages contain 14 songs that you can listen to and sing along. There are more these songs in your book, *Treasuring Your Unborn Child: Singing Treasuring Songs to Your Unborn Child.* The songs in that book are for you to hear and sing with your unborn child. First, though, you need to believe that God's love is for you, too.

For now, look through the following songs on pages 33-46. Smile as you hear and sing them. Put some joy into your voice. Just like God does, sing joyfully because you are alive. Rejoice. Be glad that God treasures and loves you. You are precious to God, and God loves <u>you</u>!

Keep this guidebook with you throughout your pregnancy and afterwards to remind yourself to sing of God's love for you.

Here's a secret. The three baby colors in this book are light purple, pink, and blue. Light purple is a combination of pink and blue. The musical notes are pink and blue on a purple staff. The color purple is a symbol of God's presence. Human beings are female and male-the pink and blue notes, arranged by God's purple staff in the concert of life.

Song Lyrics

When I Carried My Jesus

Why Listen to This Song?

More than anything else, Mary's life was defined as a mother, the Mother of Jesus. This song imagines Mary telling her experience as a mother and woman who loves her family, and your family.

Words to Sing:

When I carried my Jesus,
My mother cared for me.
A surprising Angel's visit,
Turned life into mystery.

When I carried my Jesus,
My Joseph married me.
The Angel's wondrous dream,
He hoped and thought of me.

When I carried my Jesus
My cousin called to me:
Most blessed among women
Are you destined now to be.

When I carried my Jesus,
There was trouble in our land,
We were meek and lowly
We trusted in God's hand.

When I carried my Jesus,
A donkey carried me.
To Bethlehem's noisy shack
Where my baby born would be.

When I delivered my Jesus,
I didn't know He would deliver me,
To be with Him, my God, and all
And live eternally.

When I laid down my Jesus
In swaddling cloths so snug
That He would lay down His life; broke my heart when His tomb was dug.

When I buried my Jesus,
My heart was sad and torn
Never would I have thought
This reason why He was born.

When I saw my Jesus,
Raised, alive and strong
He took me to be home with Him,
And filled my soul with song.

When I heard my Jesus,
He pledged my mother's vow:
Behold, my prayers and love are with you,
Sharing my home with you now.

The baby you now carry
Unborn, on the way to birth.
Alive and well, to belong,
To my Jesus' family on earth.

Song Lyrics

Am I Not Your Mother?

In 1531, Mary appeared to Juan Diego as Our Lady of Guadalupe. She spoke these comforting words of care with her prayers and presence to reassure him of her enduring love. Mary sings this same care for you.

Words to Sing:

Am I not your Mother,
Words I spoke so long ago
Through roses atop a mountain
And my image on a cloak.

Am I not your Mother,
When time is thick with woe
Below a mountain of worry,
That makes your spirit broke?

Am I not your Mother,
With tender, loving care
There isn't any other,
Who keeps you in constant prayer?

You, my little one, so delicate,
I am your Mother now,
To my Jesus I gave my word
To take a Mother's vow:

To hold you when you're weary,
Laugh to fill you with glee,
To walk every day with you,
In all moments make you free.

Am I not your Mother?
My little one, I am here.
My love I send you freely,
To fill your soul, my dear.

Song Lyrics

What My Mother Taught Me

Why Sing This Song?

Mary was conceived and carried in her mother's womb, like every human being is. St. Ann, Mary's mother, taught her daughter about God's love. As your mother, Mary sings her love to you.

Words to Sing:

Mothers carry mothers
The first moment in the womb
Mothers teach their daughters,
To seek their place to bloom.

Mothers join with mothers
Their life of treasured worth,
Mothers teach daughters,
To bring their best to birth.

My mother taught me wisdom.
My mother gave to God a song.
My mother told me to become,
help my children to belong.

My mother showed me sharing
With every tender touch
My mother's life was caring
Because she loves me so much.

Mothers wipe tears away
When their daughters cry
Mothers find the words to say
When their daughters ask them why.

Mothers smile, laugh, and play
When life is full of frowns,
Mothers place on daughters
A proud and graceful crown.

My mother taught me wisdom.
My mother gave to God a song.
My mother told me to become,
help my children to belong.

My mother showed me sharing
With every tender touch
My mother's life was caring
Because she loves me so much

Song Lyrics

Rose of My Heart

Why Listen to This Song?

As Our Lady of Guadalupe, Mary directed Juan Diego to pick roses which would have been out of season and present them as a sign of her request to build a church. You and your baby are the roses of Mary's heart.

Words to Sing:

Rose of my heart,
Chosen flower of mine,
Beneath Heaven's sky,
gleam in God's sunshine.

In the garden where you're growing
You blossom each day
For life beyond all knowing,
My love and prayers are coming your way.

Like grass covered with dew
We'll not be apart,
I will never leave you:
You're the rose of my heart.

Rose of my choice
Like a song on my lips
You make my heart rejoice
And all my steps skip.

From the bud in your womb
Wondrous work of art,
Your child in bloom.
Is the rose of my heart.

Rose of my heart,
You are always mine;
Beneath Heaven's sky,
gleam in God's sunshine.

For life beyond all knowing,
I send my love and prayers your way.
In God's garden you're growing,
You'll blossom every day

With devotion so true,
We'll not be apart,
I will never leave you:
You're the rose of my heart.

Song Lyrics

My Jesus Loves His Precious Ones

Why Listen to This Song?

You and your baby are precious in God's sight and in Mary's heart. Listen to this song to let their love inspire you today.

Lyrics:

Oh, my Jesus loves,
His precious ones,
His precious ones,
His precious ones,
Oh, you are His Precious Ones
To always be with Him.

Oh, I love you,
My precious ones
My precious ones,
My precious ones,
Oh yes, I love you,
My precious ones,
With my mother's heart.

Oh yes, we love
Our precious ones,
Our precious ones,
Our precious ones,
Oh yes, we love You,
Our precious ones,
Forever in God's heart.

Song Lyrics

You're My Precious Child

Why Listen to This Song?

As your spiritual mother, Mary sees your true self–a unique and precious person loved by God and her. This song reminds you of your worth as a child of God

Lyrics:

You're my precious child
Shining bright,
Alive with me,
Day and night.
When you are present,
I feel God's light,
How wondrous you are
In God's sight.

You're a marvel of grace,
Pure and true,
In every heartbeat you take,
God's love shines through.
With your life so open,
And spirit light,
You bring smiles to my eyes
You're becoming all good and right.

You're my precious child,
A joy so rare,
Living in God's presence,
With love and care.
When you are growing,
I see God's delight,
How wondrous you are
In God's sight

Song Lyrics

Ordinary Things

Why Listen to This Song:

God works slowly, in natural, ordinary things during life. This song reminds you that God's mystery is hidden in your life, yet present in ordinary ways.

Lyrics:

Through ordinary things,
In ordinary ways,
The gifts each season brings,
Bless you and your child today.

The ordinary times
When everything takes place,
My love and prayers bless you,
To fill you with God's grace.

Every day is a treasure
Moments when my heart sings
God's wonders beyond measure
Hide in ordinary things.

Glorious things unexpected,
Filled with God's surprise,
Your baby is perfected
in God's loving eyes.

Ordinary things grow slowly
Ordinary ways are sure
Ordinary times seem lowly,
Where the love of God endures.

In the mystery of a moment
God makes all things new
His gift is Heaven sent,
Life for your baby and for you

Song Lyrics

Mary's Love Song to the Unborn

Why Listen to This Song?

God's song of love resounded throughout Mary's life and spills over into the lives of all her spiritual children. Hear how her love echoes God's love for you and your family.

Words to Sing:

God sang a sweet melody
Knitting in my mother's womb.
He gave me such harmony
To grow my soul and bloom.

Inside her, God treasured me
His eyes were filled with joy.
The love that lasts eternally,
For every girl and boy.

One day, an Angel came to me,
Said I would have a Son
My heart sang magnificently
Your Will, My God, be done.

When I carried my little Jesus
I bore a new song in my soul
To sing to my dear Baby:
Who one day would make us whole.

A Song of Songs in my heart
Greets your ears today.
With all the splendid music,
My singing has to say:
God is with you every moment
And my love sings on anew:
Your baby is our present
A Christmas Day for you.

Angel chorus sang in heaven
When my baby Jesus was born
Telling all the Good News
On that first Christmas morn.

When your mother carried you,
I sang softly in her ear:
My Father, Son, my love true
Be at peace and have no fear.

For now, as you carry your baby
I'm singing a song that's new
A beautiful child of wonder
That our God is giving you.

God's melody is with you now,
Like Jesus' very first song,
He gave me to be your mother true,
To God's family you belong.

A Song of Songs in my heart
Greets your ears today.
All this love-song music
Brings Christmas home to stay.

Song Lyrics

It's a New Day to Rise and Shine

Why Sing This Song?

Admire your treasure of being with God's love, hope, and joy in a new day through you!

Words to Sing:

It's a new day to rise and shine
Rise and shine, rise and shine.
It's a new day for the Son to shine,
Shining with God's love.

It's a new day to sing a song,
Sing a song, sing a song.
It's a new day to sing along,
The hope God sings to me.

It's a new day to be in love,
Be in love, be in love.
It's a new day to see God's love
I'm precious in God's eyes.

It's a new day to dry my tears
Dry my tears, dry my tears.
It's a new day to calm my fears,
God is alive in me.

It's a new day that's full of grace
Full of grace, full of grace.
It's a new day to see God's face,
The love God has for me.

Song Lyrics

God is Blessing

Why Listen to This Song?

God blessed Mary with a life of grace, and she now prays for God's blessings on you and your unborn baby, loving you each moment. Mary loves you–all of you–all the time.

Words to Sing:

God is blessing,
God is blessing,
Loving you
All of you.
God sings a love song to you,
God brings a love song to you.
Every day,
Every day.

God is quilting
God is quilting
Covering you,
Covering you.
Feel peace in God's embracing,
You're safe in God's embracing.
God treasures you
And I do too.

God is loving
God is loving
All of you
All the time.
Yes, you are full of God's joy,
Yes, God fills you with His joy.
Made of love,
Live in love.

I am loving,
I am loving
All of you,
All the time.
You are my wondrous dearest.
My precious wondrous darling.
I love you.
I love you.
.

Song Lyrics

God Treasures Us

Why Play This Song?

Listen to these simple words about how God treasures you and your baby every day.

Words to Sing:

There's gold without refining
That paves our heart with joy;
There's silver without tarnish
That trouble can't destroy.

There's a diamond without blemish
Gleaming wondrously bright;
There are gems of every color,
Shining brilliant in God's light.

There's a field with buried treasure
waiting to be found.
There's a pearl beyond measure,
To be placed in your crown.

There's a loving God Who values
And says, "Make it thus."
For Jesus renews our lives,
Yes, our God treasures us.

Love is God's greatest treasure,
His very gift of art.
There is peace beyond measure,
When we're home within God's heart.

Song Lyrics

God Makes You So Shining New

Why Play This Song?

Reflect on these simple words of hope about God's love for you and your baby every day.

Words to Sing:

God makes you so shining new,
To share His life together.
Each joyful day, both night and day,
God lives with you forever.

In every step, and every breath,
His love is always near.
Through every joy, and every test,
God's presence calms all fear.

With gentle hands, He leads the way,
Guiding your heart so true.
Through all you face, His light will stay,
God's love renews in you.

God makes you so shining new,
His grace is ever strong.
In all you do, He's there with you,
Your heart where He belongs.

Forevermore, in peace and love,
You'll walk with Him each day.
With God above, and faith within,
You'll never lose your way.

Song Lyrics

You're My Precious Child

Why Listen to This Song?
As your spiritual mother, Mary sees your true self–a unique and precious person loved by God and her. This song reminds you of your worth as a child of God.

Lyrics:

You're my precious child
Shining bright,
Alive with me,
Day and night.
When you are present,
I feel God's light,
How wondrous you are
In God's sight.

You're a marvel of grace,
Pure and true,
In every heartbeat you take,
God's love shines through.
With your life so open,
And spirit light,
You bring smiles to my eyes
You're becoming all good and right.

You're my precious child,
A joy so rare,
Living in God's presence,
With love and care.
When you are growing,
I see God's delight,
How wondrous you are
In God's sight.

Song Lyrics

Child of Wonder

Why Listen to This Song?

Each of is God's child of wonder. Listen to these wonderful versions of the song by scanning the QR code with your mobile device. Circle the QR code of the rendition(s) that you like, so that you can play them again.

Rendition 1

Rendition 2

Rendition 3

Rendition 4

Words to Hear

<u>Refrain:</u>
You're a child of wonder,
The splendor of a dream,
that our God has sung forever,
The gift of family.

You're the dust of a star
Created from God's light
Glowing in the darkness
Radiance in bloom,
Shine in mommy's womb.

You're the seed of a song
With notes no one can hear,
Composed in the darkness,
Holy sound arise
Sing in daddy's eyes.

You're the sigh of a breath
From the Spirit paused at rest,
Knitting in the darkness,
Work of wondrous art,
Weave in Abba's heart.

You're the hope of a world
That waits upon your birth,
Dancing in the darkness.
Let all the earth rejoice:
Live in Jesus' voice.

ng:

Treasuring Your Unborn Child

Now that you have a deeper insight into how much God treasures you, you can focus on bringing that joy and peace to your unborn baby. You can treasure your baby with words and songs.

Use your pregnancy book, *Treasuring Your Unborn Child: Singing Treasuring Songs to Your Unborn Child* as a resource to talk and sing to your baby. Use the *Journal Pages* in that book to write treasuring notes to God, yourself and your unborn baby.

When you discover more things about your treasures or experience moments of God's presence, write them down in your *Journal Pages* in the book. You can write a word, a sentence, or a paragraph. It's up to you. Your pregnancy is a nine month journey. You have plenty of time to spend with God and your baby now. After your baby is born, your love will have grown much larger and stronger, too.

What's Next: Creating Your Legacy of Love

Congratulations on discovering the treasure of you during your time working with this *Guidebook*! During each day, if you keep your eyes, ears, and heart open, you will discover more wonder in your life. You will grow deeper in joy and peace. You will feel hope that life is good and getting better.

Joy is a marvelous way to live. Joy lifts your spirit, increases your gratitude, and keeps depression, sadness, and despair away. Your baby can feel your joy, which makes him/her feel safer and more secure.

Peace brings a deeper calmness to you. You feel centered and still. You are more aware, have deeper insights, and personal wisdom. Peace keeps anxiety and worry away.

Hope is the marvelous gift of the Holy Spirit assuring you that God's plan is the best one. Think and pray about this Bible verse of God speaking through the prophet Jeremiah, *"For I know well the plans I have in mind for you, plans for your welfare and not for woe, so as to give you a future of hope." Jeremiah 29:11.*

Keep This Guidebook Handy

Keep this *Guidebook* where you can reach it during your pregnancy, and after your child is born. There may be moments or days when you feel stressed or unsure of yourself. This is the time to reach for your *Guidebook* and remember your treasures. Write yourself an admiring sentence. Sing a treasuring song to yourself.

Keep your heart open to discover more about God's love in your life, your baby, and your family. Add to the *Your Three Treasures* section of this *Guidebook* as you discover more personal insights about yourself. God's love is with you every moment, every day–helping you to grow, receive God's blessings, and bless others just by being yourself. Your treasuring self.

Thank you for being the loving, lovely, and beloved woman and mother that you are. There is so much more good ahead for you in your life. Count on it! God does.

God is good: all the time. All the time: God is good. God loves me all the time.

www.ingramcontent.com/pod-product-compliance
Lightning Source LLC
LaVergne TN
LVHW070222110826
845147LV00003B/621

9781963227376